Dear Parent:

Your child's love of reading starts here!

Every child learns to read in a different way and at his or her own speed. Some go back and forth between reading levels and read favourite books again and again. Others read through each level in order. You can help your young reader improve and become more confident by encouraging his or her own interests and abilities. From books your child reads with you to the first books he or she reads alone, there are I Can Read Books for every stage of reading:

SHARED READING
Basic language, word repetition, and whimsical illustrations, ideal for sharing with your emergent reader

BEGINNING READING
Short sentences, familiar words, and simple concepts for children eager to read on their own

READING WITH HELP
Engaging stories, longer sentences, and language play for developing readers

READING ALONE
Complex plots, challenging vocabulary, and high-interest topics for the independent reader

I Can Read Books have introduced children to the joy of reading since 1957. Featuring award-winning authors and illustrators and a fabulous cast of beloved characters, I Can Read Books set the standard for beginning readers.

A lifetime of discovery begins with the magical words "I Can Read!"

Visit www.icanread.ca f(
on enriching your child's re

I Can Read Book® is a trademark of HarperCollins Publishers

Michelle Obama: First Lady and Superhero
Text copyright © 2019 by HarperCollins Publishers Ltd.
Pictures © 2019 by Nick Craine.
All rights reserved. Published by Collins, an imprint of HarperCollins Publishers Ltd.

This work is adapted from "Michelle Obama, Superhero" in *5-Minute Stories for Fearless Girls* by Sarah Howden,
illustrations by Nick Craine.

HarperCollins books may be purchased for educational, business, or sales promotional use through our Special Markets Department.

HarperCollins Publishers Ltd
Bay Adelaide Centre, East Tower
22 Adelaide Street West, 41st Floor
Toronto, Ontario, Canada
M5H 4E3

www.harpercollins.ca

Library and Archives Canada Cataloguing in Publication information is available upon request.

www.icanread.ca

ISBN 978-1-4434-5985-3

WZL 1 2 3 4 5 6 7 8 9 10

MICHELLE OBAMA:
FIRST LADY AND SUPERHERO

by Sarah Howden
pictures by Nick Craine

Collins

I was standing in front of
the White House.
It looked like a castle!

"Earth to Darlene,"

said my friend Sam.

She giggled.

"Let's pitch our tent," Sam said.

I went to help the group.

Our Girl Scout troop was
busy getting ready.
Mrs. Obama had invited us
to camp out on the lawn!

Our troop leader was Ms. Williams.

"Good job, girls," she said

when our tent was finally up.

"Mrs. Obama will be so proud,"
Ms. Williams said with a smile.
"Don't forget we will be showing
her more of our skills."

Ms. Williams turned to me.

"Darlene, will you show Mrs. Obama how to tie a square knot?"

My stomach flipped like a pancake.

Then it flopped like a fish.

"No, thank you," I said.

Ms. Williams looked at me.

"Will you think about it?" she said.

Then she walked away to help

some other girls out.

"I don't get it," Sam said.

"You're great with knots."

"Usually I am," I said.

"But I don't want to mess up
in front of Mrs. Obama."
Sam shrugged.

"I can't wait to meet the
First Lady," Sam said.
"My mom said she's why I have
free lunches at school."

16

"So now my stomach isn't grumbling through science class!" Sam grinned.

"I heard Mrs. Obama is helping girls
around the world stay in school,"
I said.
"And that she met Elmo from
Sesame Street!"

"Mrs. Obama is like a superhero,"
Sam said.

"It's time, girls!"
called Ms. Williams.

My stomach flipped again.

We all went to sit in a circle.

Then Mrs. Obama arrived.

I thought she looked like a queen.

Mrs. Obama sat down on a hay bale.

"Welcome to all of you," she said.

"I'm so excited you're here."

"This is the first time anyone has camped on this lawn,"
Mrs. Obama said.
"You're making history!"

We all cheered.

"I remember when I was a kid,"
Mrs. Obama said.
"I was smart and I always
tried my best."

"But I worried a lot.

I worried about messing things up."

Sam looked over at me.

"Some people told me I wasn't
good enough. That didn't help,"
Mrs. Obama said.

"I wish I could tell that little girl to have faith in herself," Mrs. Obama said. "And that it's okay to make mistakes."

"Now I'm looking forward to meeting each of you!" Mrs. Obama said. "You can show me your stuff!"

Sam reached over and
squeezed my hand.
"You should have faith
in yourself too," she said.

"Will you come with me?" I asked.

Sam nodded.

"Ms. Williams?" I said.

"Can I still show Mrs. Obama

my square knot?"

"Come with me!" she said.

I didn't get it right at first.

But that was okay.

Mrs. Obama gave me a high-five.

She knew I'd tried my very best.